THE EARLY CRETACEOUS:
VOLUME 2

NOTES, DRAWINGS, AND OBSERVATIONS FROM PREHISTORY

BY JUAN CARLOS ALONSO & GREGORY S. PAUL

*For Dali, may you never lose
your sense of wonder.
Love, Dad.*

This library edition published in 2017 by Walter Foster Jr.,
an imprint of The Quarto Group
6 Orchard Road, Suite 100
Lake Forest, CA 92630

Distributed in the United States and Canada by
Lerner Publisher Services
241 First Avenue North
Minneapolis, MN 55401 U.S.A.
www.lernerbooks.com

First Library Edition

Library of Congress Cataloging-in-Publication Data

Names: Alonso, Juan Carlos (Graphic designer), author, illustrator. | Paul, Gregory S., author.
Title: The early Cretaceous / by Juan Carlos Alonso & Gregory S. Paul.
Other titles: Ancient Earth journal.
Description: First library edition. | Lake Forest, CA : Walter Foster Jr., an
  imprint of Quarto Publishing Group USA Inc., 2017. | Series: Ancient Earth
  journal | Audience: Ages 8+. | Includes bibliographical references and index.
Identifiers: LCCN 2017011684 | ISBN 9781942875307 (volume 1 : hardcover : alk.
  paper) | ISBN 9781942875314 (volume 2 : hardcover : alk. paper)
Subjects: LCSH: Paleontology--Cretaceous--Juvenile literature. |
  Dinosaurs--Juvenile literature. | Animals, Fossil--Juvenile literature. |
  CYAC: Prehistoric animals.
Classification: LCC QE861.5 .A427 2017 | DDC 560.177--dc23
LC record available at https://lccn.loc.gov/2017011684

Printed in USA
9 8 7 6 5 4 3 2 1

Table of Contents

Forewords

Philip J. Currie, MSc, PhD, FRSC
Professor and Canada Research Chair, Dinosaur Paleobiology
University of Alberta, Edmonton, Canada

O nce a dark period in the geological history of the Earth, the Early Cretaceous is rapidly becoming one of the best-understood periods of the Mesozoic Era (often called the Age of Reptiles). The Early Cretaceous is bracketed between the spectacular Late Jurassic and Late Cretaceous periods; fossil-bearing sites suggest huge changes took place in the faunas and floras during this time. In short, major transformations took place in the Early Cretaceous that signaled the beginning of the modern world. Over the last two decades, incredible fossils from this time period have been found all over the world.

Driven by the origin and rise of flowering plants, environments were starting to become more "modern" in appearance, promoting the evolution of insects, lizards, snakes, dinosaurs, birds, and mammals at unprecedented rates. However, it would still be more than 50 million years before non-avian dinosaurs would die out, along with flying reptiles and so many other animals.

As a palaeontologist who works mostly with Late Cretaceous dinosaurs, I would love to climb into a time machine and be transported back a hundred million years or so. Sitting in an Early Cretaceous forest with my pencil and notebook, camera, and sketchbook, I would try to understand the big changes that were imminent—dinosaurs were about to go into their last great flowering, with very different things happening in the northern and southern hemispheres. I would keep my eyes open for the dangerous dinosaurs, of course, especially predators such as the dog-sized Deinonychus and the giant Acrocanthosaurus. (That might be hard to do, however, because it would be so fascinating to watch the little feathered theropods like the Microraptor hunting lizards, mammals, and birds, while flocks of essentially modern birds mixed with more primitive toothed or long-tailed relatives!)

Although it will never be possible for me to travel physically back to that wonderful time, *The Early Cretaceous* has the feel of a naturalist's notebook to conjure up such illusions and dreams. I hope these wonderful images have the same effect on you!

Matthew T. Mossbrucker

Director & Chief Curator

Morrison Natural History Museum, Morrison, Colorado

So that's what they think dinosaurs looked like? I have seen this scenario play out in museum exhibits on scores of occasions. Curious visitors introduced to life history via art. This synergy between paleontologists, who are charged with the study of fossil life forms, and specially trained artists is vital for intuitively communicating past life on earth.

Those of us who are charged with interpreting fossils for the masses have come to rely on this special type of artist, the "paleoartist," to help us resurrect animals and plants from the deep recesses of time. Paleoartists are the unsung heroes of science literacy. Their vital skills translate the inanimate remains of long-dead creatures once again into living beasts. They inspire a connection between our world and the countless ecosystems that have come and gone before us.

Perhaps nothing stirs the imagination like dinosaurs—monstrous and exotic forms brought to life through the imagination of artistic scientists like Juan Carlos Alonso and Gregory S. Paul. This book is a wonderful blend of imagination and reality and a testament to the powerful partnership between art and science.

Cycad plants and leaf detail

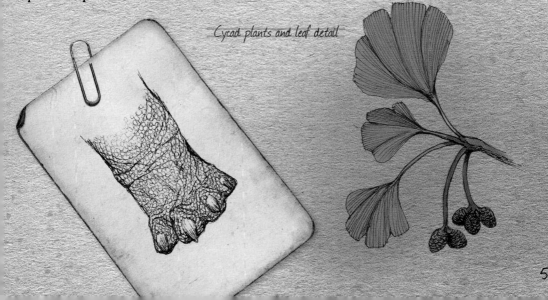

Introduction

I magine stepping back in time 120 million years to the Early Cretaceous period and walking around on an earth similar to today's, yet in many regards, almost alien.

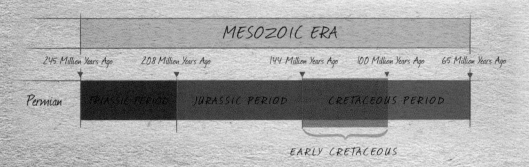

The Early Cretaceous is the last period of the Mesozoic Era, or "the age of the reptiles." The earth is undergoing monumental changes; the once giant supercontinent is slowly drifting apart. The tectonic plates are tearing apart along a great fiery rift, forming the early North Atlantic Ocean. South America and Africa are still partly attached to one another, while close by Antarctica, Australia, and India are bundled into one continent.

A massive shallow sea covers large areas, turning Europe into an archipelago of islands similar to today's Indonesia. The great tropical Tethys Ocean divides Asia from the southern continents and the vast Pacific Ocean is the largest it will ever be.

As you travel through the Early Cretaceous, you will experience warm temperatures throughout most of the world. Seasons consist of a dry and a wet period. Approaching the poles, winters are dark and very cold. You will see glaciers gracing some highlands, especially in the southernmost areas. As you cross the center of the continents, you will encounter endless arid deserts, making your journey difficult, if not impossible. Areas of abundant plant life are widespread, with the ground covered in waist-high ferns forming broad prairies in drier flatlands.

As you travel through forests, you will see short cycads, gingko trees, and enormous canopies of towering conifers. Small flowering shrubs—the first to appear on the earth—decorate the banks of streams and creeks. You can't walk through fields of grass nor can you see hardwood trees, including oak or walnut, as they haven't evolved yet. A lot of the animal life will look familiar to you. Small bodies of water are home to frogs, turtles, and salamanders.

You might find lizards and rodent-sized mammals scurrying through the underbrush as well as burrowing into the ground. The insects look familiar too; you will spot dragonflies, flies, fleas, roaches, social termites, wasps, and moths. In many ways,

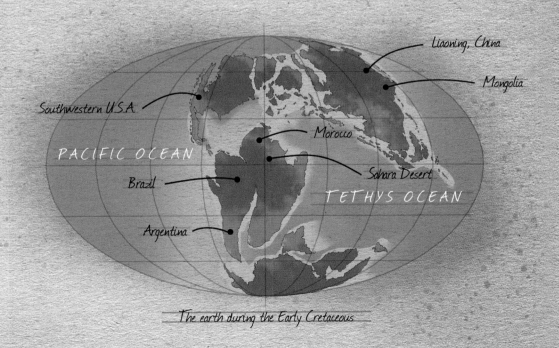

The earth during the Early Cretaceous

the Early Cretaceous will remind you of several places on earth today. But in other ways, it is an incredibly different world.

Much of the wildlife of the Early Cretaceous period is simply extraordinary! Animals have adapted for survival in a dinosaur-dominated environment so savage that it's unsafe for people to move about unless they are armed.

Deadly two-legged, long-tailed predators the length of a city bus and swifter than any human roam freely, each capable of swallowing a man whole. (It's no wonder that some herbivorous dinosaurs are armored like tanks!) Others are land whales weighing up to 100 tons and measuring five stories tall! These creatures move in huge herds, wrecking the umbrella-shaped conifers they feed upon. Yet other big herbivorous dinosaurs look like crosses between massive cattle and ducks, with flat beaks designed for tearing into plants.

Not all of the Early Cretaceous dinosaurs are big, however. In fact, most are fairly small and often feathered like birds. Most of the small dinosaurs are beaked plant-eaters and fast on their two legs. Many are bipedal predators. Some have sickle-shaped razor claws on their inner toes used to disembowel their prey. The dinosaurs most closely related to birds have wings on both of their arms and legs that they use to fly between trees and pounce on prey from above. Birds as we now know them today are just beginning to appear. They often live in enormous flocks, giving some

Pinecones

Conifer branch and needles

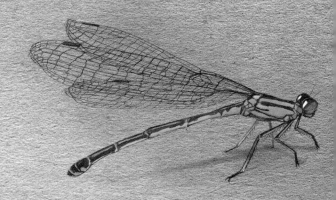

stiff competition to the flying pterosaurs that had long ruled the skies. Pterosaurs are growing larger, sporting enormous head crests and shorter tails.

Now imagine living alongside these animals, recording and sketching every possible detail of their lives in your journal. The premise of this book is to bring these magnificent animals to life for you through art and science. Discover the Early Cretaceous world and its life through new eyes, and get to know the personalities of each species. Discover how sauropods with heads five stories above the ground could pump blood to their brains under extreme pressures. Discover how dinosaurs learned to fly as they developed wings. See how some dinosaurs survived polar blizzards, while others lived through desert heat. This journal gives you a visual guide to what it must have been like to experience possibly the strangest wildlife the earth has ever seen and may never see again.

Welcome to the Early Cretaceous.

The Sauropods

As you walk through the Early Cretaceous landscape, you find yourself near a clearing in the trees. Just ahead of you is a dry lake bed. You look up and notice you are ankle-high with an animal as tall as a building and as wide as a whale! The earth trembles as the creature drops its massive foot to the ground. Around you there are hundreds of these animals walking together in a great herd across the landscape looking for food. Their massive necks are slowly swaying forward with each step. You feel the constant rumble under your feet and hear sporadic trumpeting as if announcing their arrival. You are in the presence of true giants, the largest animals to ever walk the earth—the sauropods.

Sauropods were an extraordinary group of dinosaurs belonging to the saurischian family, named for the lizard-like structure of their hips. The name sauropod, meaning "lizard-footed" in Greek, was given to these animals in 1878 by paleontologist O.C. Marsh upon discovering their huge legs and feet. Their long necks and whip-like tails made them easy to recognize. All of them stood on four legs, some reaching lengths of over 100 feet (30 meters) and weighing more than 50 tons. (That's longer than any animal that has ever lived, including the blue whale!) The very first sauropod species appeared in the late Triassic Period.

6 feet

3 feet

Its descendants thrived until the end of the age of dinosaurs, about 150 million years—by far the most successful herbivorous group of land animals in history. By the late Jurassic Period, sauropods filled the landscape with great thunderous herds of Brachiosaurs, Diplodocus, and other enormous species stretching as far as the eye could see. They dominated the land; this was the time of giants. The sauropods continued to evolve into diverse species through the Early Cretaceous, giving us some of the largest and most fascinating animals that ever existed.

Sauropods' bodies were rather short in comparison to their necks and tails. Their legs were thick, sturdy, and strong, similar to an elephant's. They supported the weight of their massive necks and tails through tall spines in their backbones, which acted much like a suspension bridge, allowing both the neck and tail to swing independently while anchored to the body. Some had tails as long as their necks and bodies combined. They would use their tails as immense whips swaying constantly, protecting their hindquarters from attack. Some had upright necks that extended 70 feet into the air, as tall as a 7-story building. In order to pump blood to their heads, sauropods developed massive hearts and a network of blood vessels complete with valves that prevented blood from flowing back down due to the force of gravity. This enabled them to maintain blood pressure whether eating from the treetops or drinking from the ground.

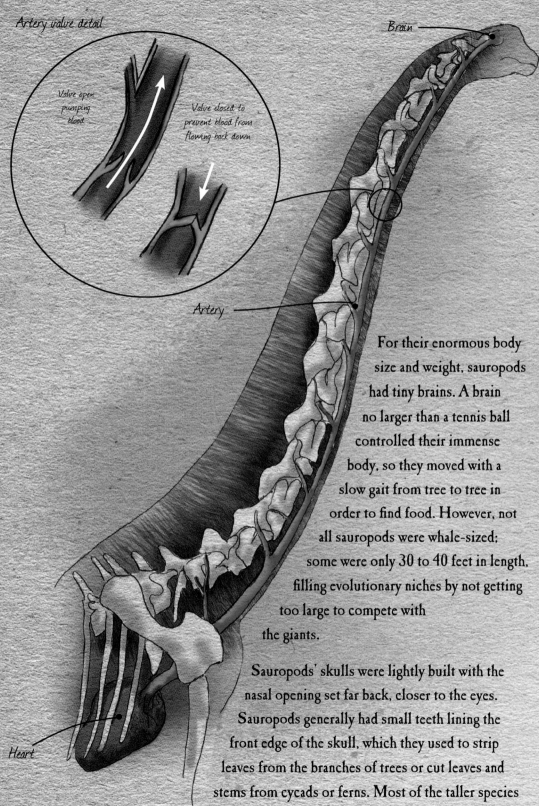

Artery valve detail

Valve open pumping blood

Valve closed to prevent blood from flowing back down

Brain

Artery

Heart

For their enormous body size and weight, sauropods had tiny brains. A brain no larger than a tennis ball controlled their immense body, so they moved with a slow gait from tree to tree in order to find food. However, not all sauropods were whale-sized; some were only 30 to 40 feet in length, filling evolutionary niches by not getting too large to compete with the giants.

Sauropods' skulls were lightly built with the nasal opening set far back, closer to the eyes. Sauropods generally had small teeth lining the front edge of the skull, which they used to strip leaves from the branches of trees or cut leaves and stems from cycads or ferns. Most of the taller species fed on pine needles and cones from towering conifer trees. None had developed larger teeth for chewing, so all the plant matter was directly swallowed and deposited into their immense stomachs. Most would swallow small stones or gastroliths to grind the plant matter within the stomach.

The Sauropods of the Early Cretaceous

Throughout the Jurassic Period, many species became larger to outgrow the predators that hunted them. They became so large that an adult sauropod had no known enemies! No animal could withstand the force of a healthy sauropod weighing 80 to 100 tons, so size was a means of survival for the species. This was evident in the Early Cretaceous Period as well, with species like Argentinosaurus huinculensis and Sauroposeidon proteles, two of the largest sauropods to ever live. They were unimaginably large, yet they were born from eggs less than 8 inches in diameter (about the size of a volleyball).

A newborn was small enough to fit in one of your hands and later grew to be several thousand times its own size at maturity, unlike any animal on earth today. (Imagine an elephant hatching from a chicken's egg!)

Though their size was truly impressive, it was their distinct adaptations that made the sauropods so unique in the Early Cretaceous Period. Animals like the Nigersaurus taqueti developed an odd skull with a flat mouth, designed to eat parallel to the ground so it could maximize the amount of food with each bite. The front of its mouth was lined with 500 thin teeth, each sliding into the opposing tooth to act like a pair of shears, cutting ferns and cycads swiftly with each bite. The Amargasaurus cazaui was equally as strange; it developed a large crest with long spines protruding from its neck vertebrae to deter its predators and attract mates.

In the following pages we will take a look at how diversified the sauropods became in the Early Cretaceous Period. You'll get close enough to examine these extraordinary animals in fine detail, witnessing their impressive size and fascinating adaptations.

Amargasaurus cazaui

Location Observed: La Amarga, Argentina

Family: Dicraeosauridae

Length: 43 feet (15 meters)

Height: 8 feet (2.5 meters)

Weight: 6 tons

Temperament: Social, reclusive

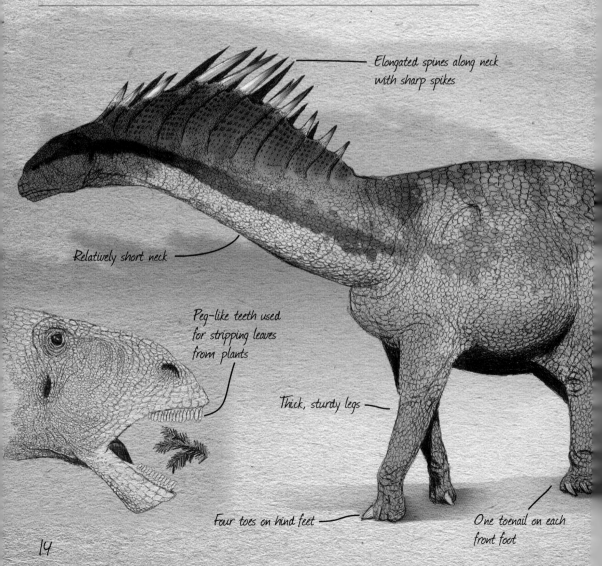

Elongated spines along neck with sharp spikes

Relatively short neck

Peg-like teeth used for stripping leaves from plants

Thick, sturdy legs

Four toes on hind feet

One toenail on each front foot

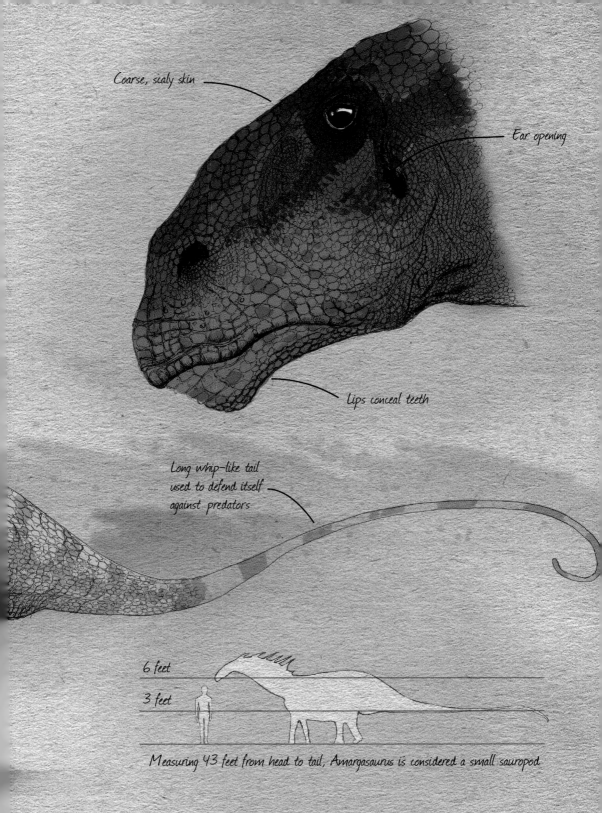

Coarse, scaly skin

Ear opening

Lips conceal teeth

Long whip-like tail
used to defend itself
against predators

6 feet

3 feet

Measuring 43 feet from head to tail, Amargasaurus is considered a small sauropod

Argentinosaurus huinculensis

Long head

Neck capable of
reaching both
tall trees and the
ground to feed

Long, flexible neck

Longer forelimbs

Location Observed: Huincul, Argentina

Family: Antarctosauridae

Length: 100 feet (30 meters)

Height: 60 feet (20 meters)

Weight: Over 50 tons

Temperament: Social, slow moving

Argentinosaurus is one of the largest animals
to ever walk the earth

6 feet

3 feet

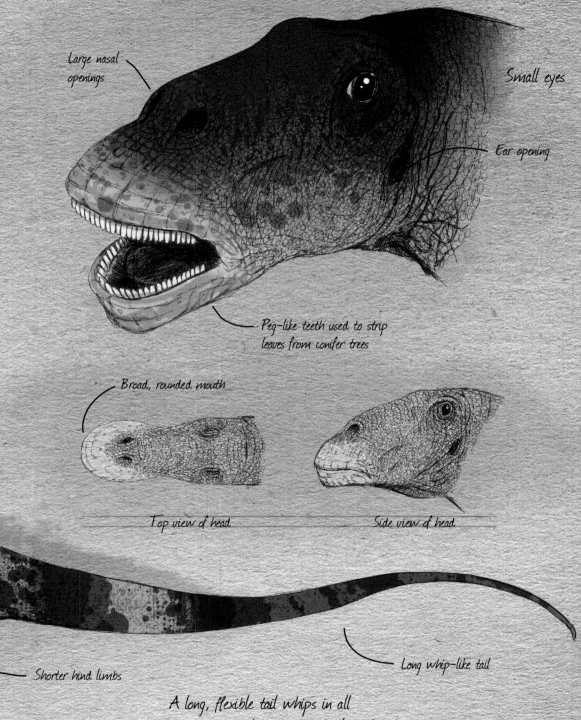

Large nasal openings

Small eyes

Ear opening

Peg-like teeth used to strip leaves from conifer trees

Broad, rounded mouth

Top view of head

Side view of head

Shorter hind limbs

Long whip-like tail

A long, flexible tail whips in all directions, making it impossible to attack from behind

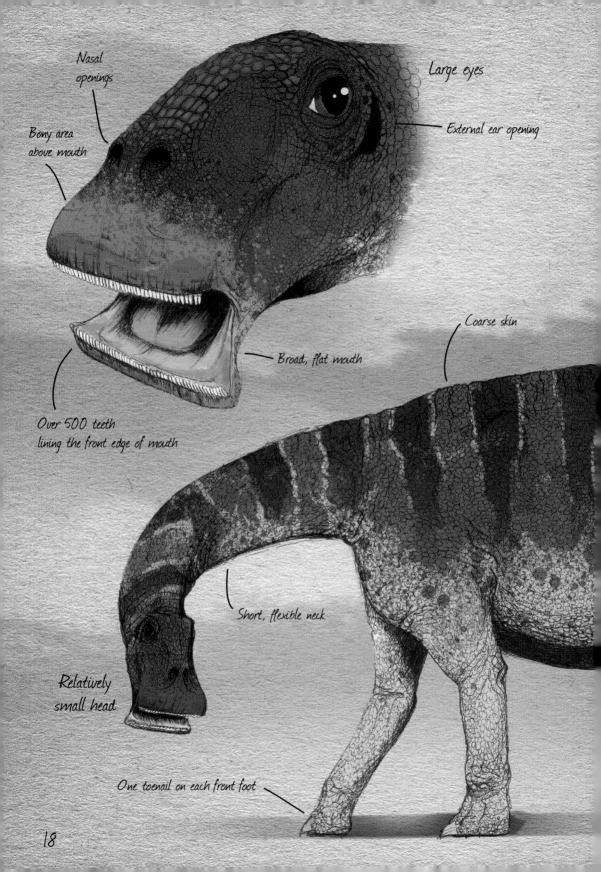

Nasal
openings

Large eyes

Bony area
above mouth

External ear opening

Coarse skin

Broad, flat mouth

Over 500 teeth
lining the front edge of mouth

Short, flexible neck

Relatively
small head

One toenail on each front foot

Nigersaurus taqueti

Location Observed: *Gadoufaoua, Republic of Niger*

Family: *Rebbachisauridae*

Length: *30 feet (9 meters)*

Height: *7 feet (2.2 meters)*

Weight: *2 tons*

Temperament: *Solitary, shy*

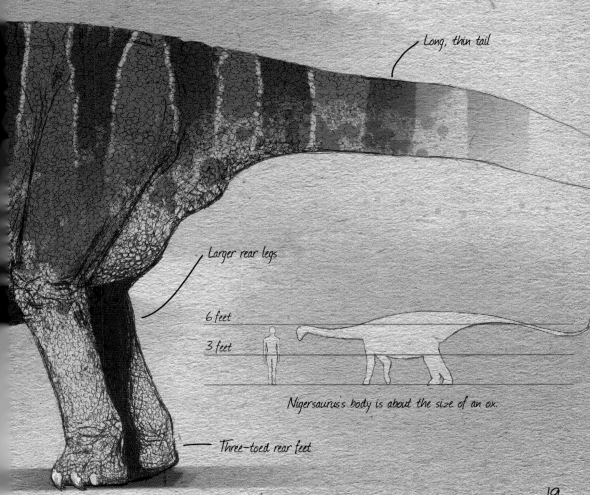

Long, thin tail

Larger rear legs

6 feet

3 feet

Nigersaurus's body is about the size of an ox.

Three-toed rear feet

Long, thin, whip-like tail acts as a defense
to protect its hindquarters

Nigersaurus rears on its hind legs
when threatened

Forelimbs used to
defend itself

Lightly built skull positioned facing downward

Bottom and top teeth interlock to act like shears. Worn teeth are constantly replaced by new teeth.

Plants are sheared off with each bite, leaving only stumps

Nigersaurus eats mostly horsetail plants and ferns

Sauroposeidon proteles

Location Observed: *Oklahoma, United States*

Family: *Brachiosauridae*

Length: *90 feet (27 meters)*

Height: *60 feet (18 meters)*

Weight: *40 tons*

Temperament: *Social, territorial*

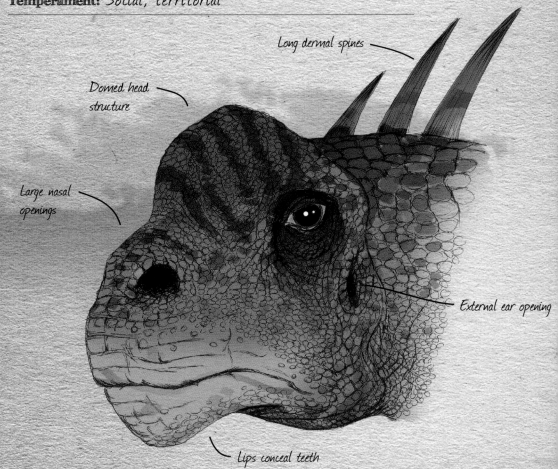

Long dermal spines

Domed head structure

Large nasal openings

External ear opening

Lips conceal teeth

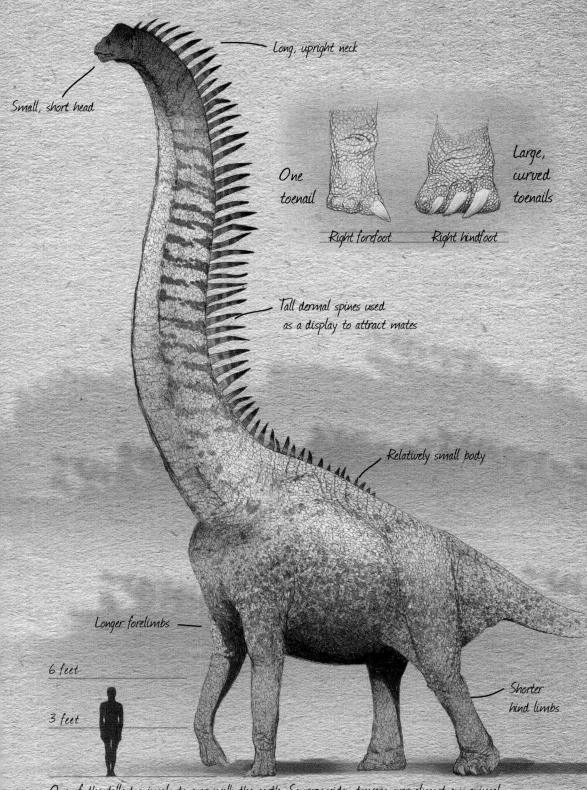

Long, upright neck

Small, short head

One toenail

Large, curved toenails

Right forefoot

Right hindfoot

Tall dermal spines used as a display to attract mates

Relatively small body

Longer forelimbs

6 feet

3 feet

Shorter hind limbs

One of the tallest animals to ever walk the earth, Sauroposeidon towers over almost any animal

The Ornithischians

You gaze across the Early Cretaceous landscape and see tall conifer trees in the distance with a field of fern and cycad plants before you. The weather is muggy and hot with sounds of insects and birds filling the air. The scenery is dotted with groups of large animals, about the size of elephants, slowly walking, then momentarily breaking stride to eat. Like modern-day antelope, they take turns raising their heads looking for potential danger. They continue on their way without much bother. Soon four armored animals join the group. They are lower to the ground but just as massive, all of them grazing on the plants beneath them. As one would come to expect, things don't remain calm for very long in the Cretaceous. All the animals become restless, some begin to make noise as they gather into a herd. A pack of six theropods have been hunting them. Now in the open, they are in plain sight for the herd to see. The herd is tightly grouped and moving as if it were one animal. The theropods begin to charge in hopes of disbanding them, but they stay together leaving the theropods no

6 feet

3 feet

option but to abandon the attack. Eventually, calm is restored as they all return to grazing. This is a typical day in the Early Cretaceous, and what it must have been like to be large prey, more specifically an ornithischian.

Ornithischians, meaning "bird-hipped," are an extremely diverse group of herbivorous dinosaurs characterized by their hip structure and beaks at the front of their jaws. They come in many forms—from large duck-billed animals resembling cattle to small parrot-like lizards to heavily armored walking fortresses. Because of this diversity, ornithischians are divided into three subgroups: thyreophorans, which include armored dinosaurs; heterodontosaurs, which include the horned and frilled dinosaurs; and ornithopods, which include duck-billed dinosaurs.

The first ornithischians evolved in the Late Triassic and continued to thrive until the end of the Mesozoic, making them one of the most successful groups of plant-eating

dinosaurs. All have hard beaks designed for snipping and cutting plants, while most have jaws lined with closely placed, leaf-shaped teeth used for grinding plant matter. Many in the species are exclusively quadrupeds. Some are capable of easily transitioning between moving on four legs and standing or running on two.

The Ornithischians of the Early Cretaceous

The Early Cretaceous is a transitory time for the ornithischians, seeing the emergence of species like Iguanodon bernissartensis, which are spreading across many continents. These are the great ancestors of what will soon be the hadrosaurs, or duck-billed dinosaurs. The Late Cretaceous sees the rise of the hadrosaur family as they flourish into an array of species, some with hollow crests and ornamental growths, and others that are larger and bulkier.

The Early Cretaceous is also a turning point for the ceratopsians. Species like Psittacosaurus mongoliensis, prolific in their numbers, are developing and are the ancestors to the great horned dinosaur: Triceratops.

This section delves into the diversity of ornithischians, with each of the three subgroups represented by key species that define the era.

Closely placed teeth for
grinding plant matter

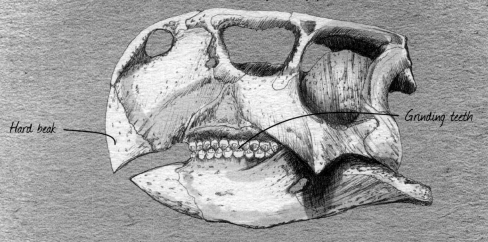

Hard beak

Grinding teeth

Psittacosaurus mongoliensis skull

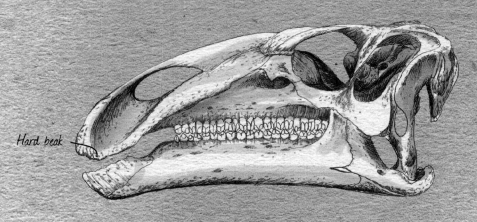

Hard beak

Iguanodon bernissartensis skull

Gastonia burgei

Location Observed: *Utah, United States*

Family: *Nodosauridae*

Length: *17 feet (5 meters)*

Height: *4 feet (1.3 meters)*

Weight: *1.9 tons*

Temperament: *Aggressive, solitary*

Thick, bony plates on back serve as armor

Wide, flat body

Short, sturdy legs

6 feet

3 feet

Gastonia weighs as much as a rhinoceros

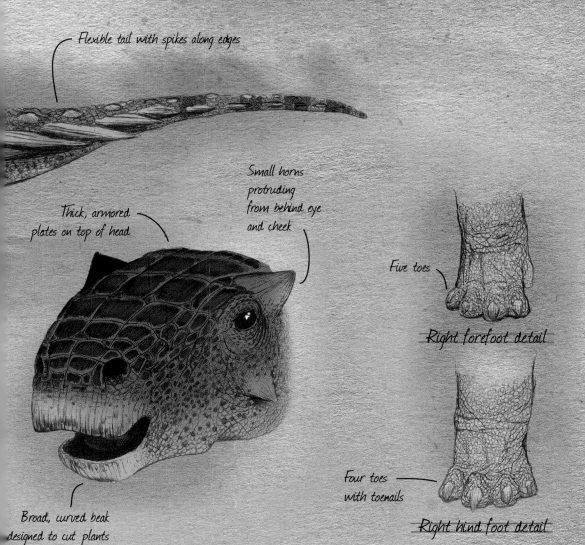

Flexible tail with spikes along edges

Thick, armored plates on top of head

Small horns protruding from behind eye and cheek

Five toes

Right forefoot detail

Broad, curved beak designed to cut plants

Four toes with toenails

Right hind foot detail

Iguanodon bernissartensis

Location Observed: *Utah, United States*

Family: *Iguanodontidae*

Length: *26 feet (8 meters)*

Height: *7 feet (2.1 meters)*

Weight: *3.2 tons*

Temperament: *Cautious, social*

Long, flexible neck

Thick, powerful legs

Larger hind limbs

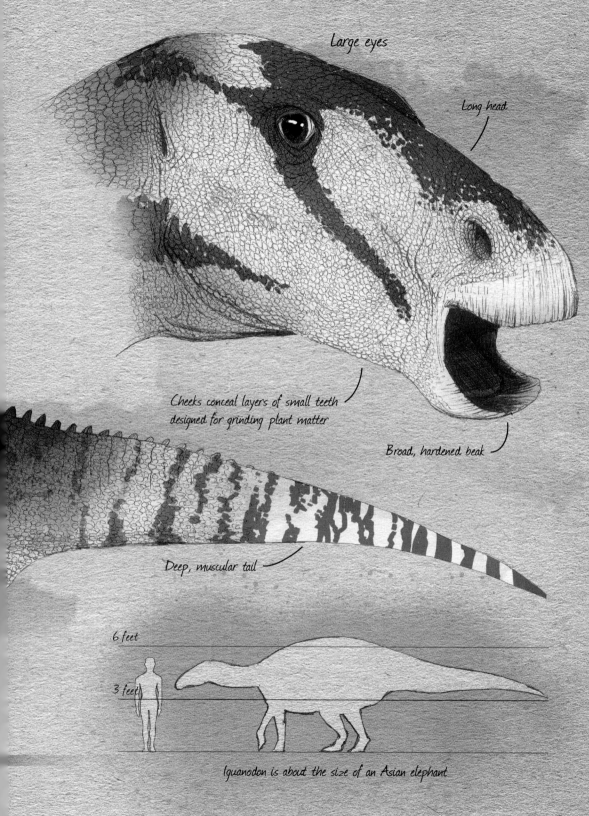

Large eyes

Long head

Cheeks conceal layers of small teeth
designed for grinding plant matter

Broad, hardened beak

Deep, muscular tail

6 feet

3 feet

Iguanodon is about the size of an Asian elephant

Primarily a quadruped walking
on all fours, but can walk and
run on two legs

Iguanodons live in large, familial herds
consisting of several generations

Iguanodons feed
mostly on low-
growing plants

Broad, large hind feet with long toes

Small, flexible toe on outside of foot

Large "thumb" spike used as a defensive weapon

Right foot detail

Right hand detail

Row of dermal spines appear once mature

The young stay close to the adults for protection

Ouranosaurus nigeriensis

Location Observed: Niger, Africa

Family: Iguanodontidae

Length: 27 feet (8.3 meters)

Height: 10.5 feet (3.2 meters)

Weight: 2.2 tons

Temperament: Social, cautious

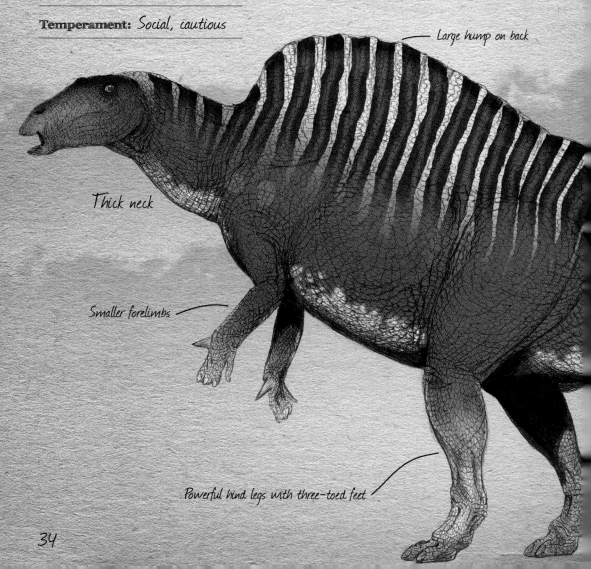

Large hump on back

Thick neck

Smaller forelimbs

Powerful hind legs with three-toed feet

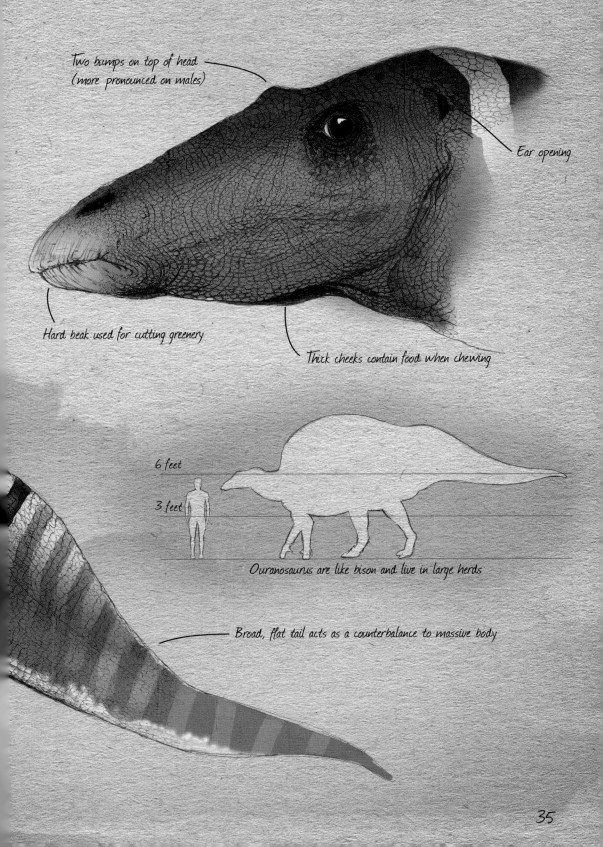

Two bumps on top of head
(more pronounced on males)

Ear opening

Hard beak used for cutting greenery

Thick cheeks contain food when chewing

6 feet

3 feet

Ouranosaurus are like bison and live in large herds

Broad, flat tail acts as a counterbalance to massive body

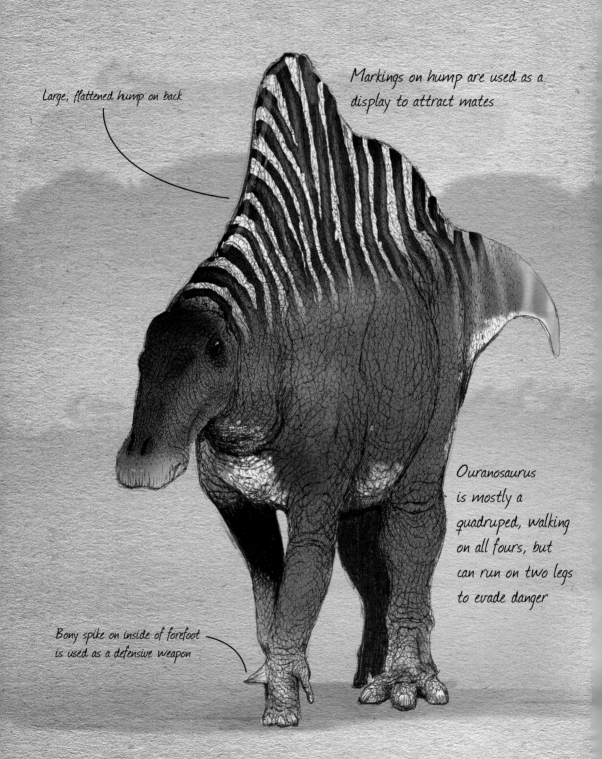

Large, flattened hump on back

Markings on hump are used as a display to attract mates

Ouranosaurus is mostly a quadruped, walking on all fours, but can run on two legs to evade danger

Bony spike on inside of forefoot is used as a defensive weapon

"Thumb" spike

Small, underdeveloped, flexible toe on outside of foot

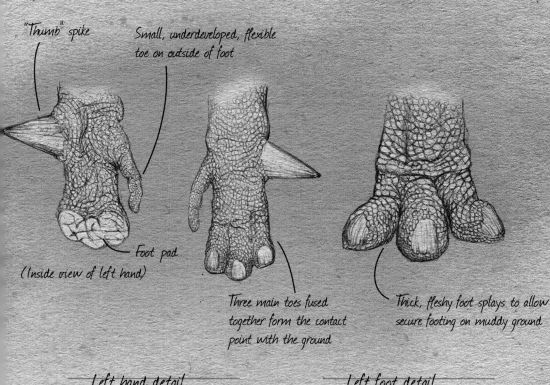

Foot pad
(Inside view of left hand)

Three main toes fused together form the contact point with the ground

Thick, fleshy foot splays to allow secure footing on muddy ground

Left hand detail   Left foot detail

They live in large herds. The young never leave the group.

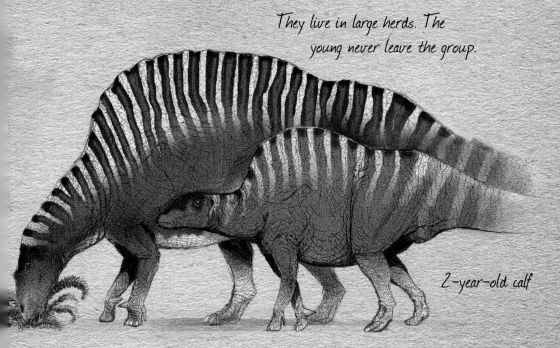

2-year-old calf

Feeds mostly on ferns and cycads

Psittacosaurus mongoliensis

Location Observed: Gobi Desert, Mongolia

Family: Ceratopsian

Length: 5 feet (1.5 meters)

Height: 2 feet (.8 meters)

Weight: 35 lbs (15kg)

Temperament: Cautious, very social

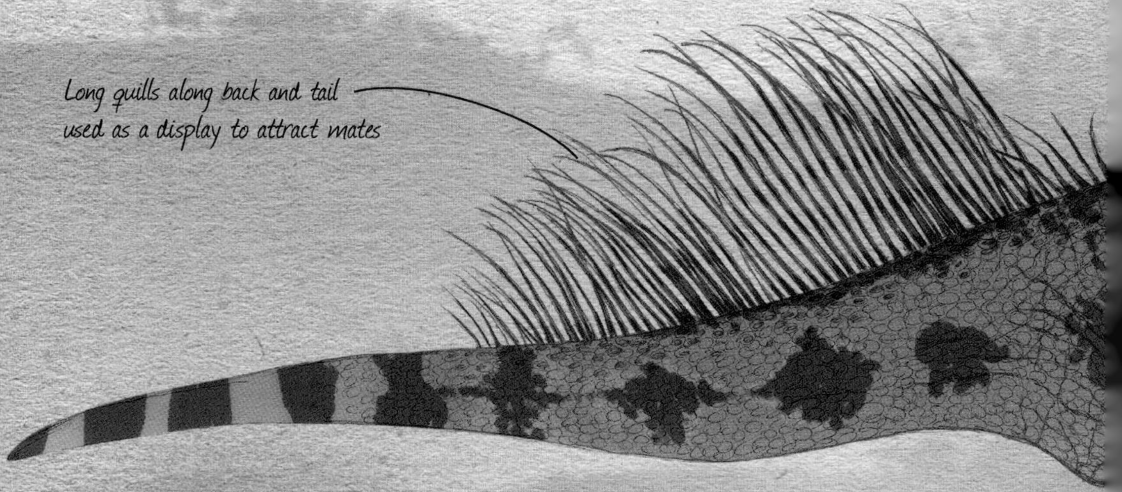

Long quills along back and tail used as a display to attract mates

6 feet

3 feet

Strong hind limbs, capable of walking and standing on two legs

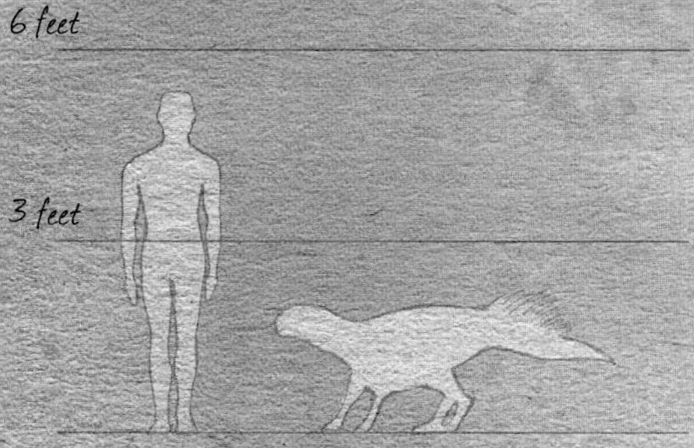

The adult Psittacosaurus is the size of a dog

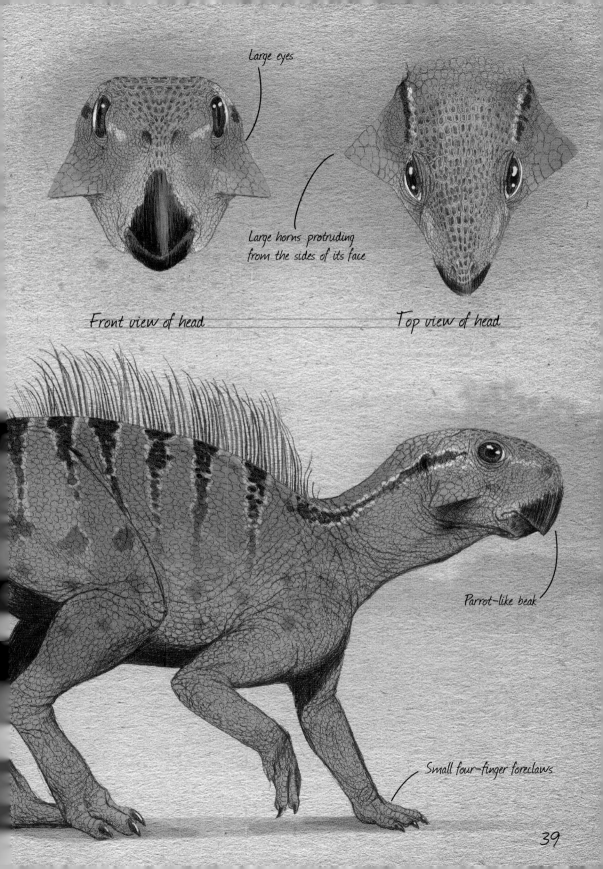

Large eyes

Large horns protruding
from the sides of its face

Front view of head

Top view of head

Parrot-like beak

Small four-finger foreclaws

39

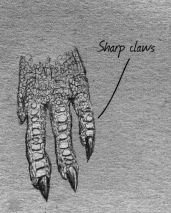

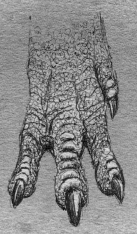

Sharp claws

Right foreclaw   Right hind foot

Psittacosaurus live in small family packs and spend most of their time together foraging for food

Back quills are absent in females

Pebbly skin

Hard beak used to cut plants and leaves
into small pieces

Fleshy cheeks conceal teeth
for grinding plants

At two months old, they are about the size
of a rabbit and capable of evading predators

The First Birds

Imagine being a bird watcher in the Early Cretaceous. Looking up, you see the skies swarming with small birds. Along coastlines and waterways, you observe what look like flightless waterfowl floating on the surface, diving down momentarily, then popping back up with fish in their mouths. Overhead, flying alongside the pterosaurs, are birds much like modern seagulls or terns competing for fish. Considering the strange wildlife of the period, surprisingly, these birds look very similar to today's birds. Many act much like modern birds as well—jumping from branch to branch, chirping, eating seeds, and hunting small insects. These are early birds–not bird-like dinosaurs–with their own distinctive class. While the appearance may remind you of a finch or a crow, there are key differences. Most of these early birds have clawed hands on their wings and many still display teeth on their beaks, all vestiges of their ancestors, the theropod dinosaurs.

It is in the Early Cretaceous that birds really make their mark on earth. While still archaic, bird species advance rapidly and begin to distinguish themselves from their dino-bird lineage. Their tails begin to disappear and wings become fuller and larger. Birds streamline the process of flying by developing feathers that contour to the shape of the body, making them more aerodynamic. Teeth get smaller and, in some species, disappear completely in favor of lighter beaks. The loss of their ancestors' long

tails allows for dynamic flight and increased maneuverability in the air—an adaptation that is still visible in today's birds.

This section looks at two contrasting species: one an adept flier abundant in the Early Cretaceous skies; the other a toothed, flightless waterbird with adaptations for aquatic hunting. You'll notice the similarities right away, but look closely and you will see the remaining hints of their common ancestry with the dinosaurs.

Confuciusornis sanctus

Location Observed: Liaoning, China

Family: Confuciusornithidae

Length: 2.3 feet (.7 meters) wingspan

Height: 9 inches (22 centimeters) body length

Weight: .39 pounds (180 grams)

Temperament: Highly social

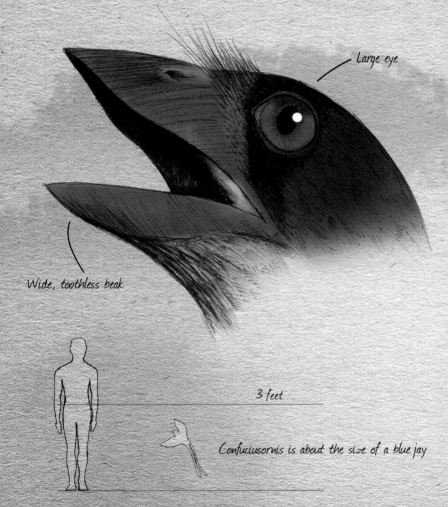

Large eye

Wide, toothless beak

3 feet

Confuciusornis is about the size of a blue jay

Two long feathers
to attract mates

Male Confuciusornis

Female Confuciusornis

Three claws on wing

Primary flight feathers
extremely long compared to
modern birds

Wing detail (underside)

45

Enaliornis barretti

Location Observed: London, England

Family: Enaliornithidae

Length: 1 foot (.3 meters) body

Height: 5 inches (12.7 centimeters) body width

Weight: 1 pound (.45 kilograms)

Temperament: Solitary, elusive

Long beak lined with small teeth used to catch fish

Small throat pouch

3 feet

Enaliornis is about the size of a large pigeon

Short tail

When diving for fish,
Enaliornis positions legs
and feet in a wide stance

Small, atrophied wings

Left foot detail

Lobed toes
for propulsion
in water

47

Pronunciation Key

Sauropods (Sore-uh-pods)
Amargasaurus cazaui (Ah-mahr-ga-sore-us, kaz-aw-ee)
Argentinosaurus huinculensis (Are-jen-tee-no-sore-us, june-kull-en-sis)
Nigersaurus taqueti (Knee-ja-sore-us, ta-ket-tee)
Sauroposeidon proteles (Sore-o-poe-side-un, pro-tell-ease)

Ornithischians (Ore-ni-thisk-key-ahns)
Gastonia burgei (Gass-toe-ni-ah, burr-gee)
Iguanodon bernissartensis (Igg-wan-oh-don, bur-nis-sar-ten-sis)
Ouranosaurus nigeriensis (Ew-ron-o-sore-us, nie-jeer-ee-en-sis]
Psittacosaurus mongoliensis (See-taco-sore-us, mon-go-lee-nen-sis)

Birds
Confuciusornis sanctus (Con-few-shus-or-nis, sank-tus)
Enaliornis barretti (En-al-lee-or-nis, bar-rett-tee)

About the Authors

Juan Carlos Alonso
Juan Carlos Alonso (author and illustrator) is a Cuban American graphic designer, creative director, and illustrator. He has over 30 years experience in the graphic design/illustration field. In 1992 he founded Alonso & Company, a creative boutique specializing in branding, design, and advertising. His passion for nature has taken him around the world, from Australia to the Galapagos Islands, to study animals. Along with his work in the graphic arts, he is also an accomplished wildlife sculptor, focusing mostly on prehistoric animals.

Gregory S. Paul
Gregory S. Paul (co-author) is an American freelance researcher, author, and illustrator who works in paleontology. He is best known for his work and research on theropod dinosaurs and his detailed illustrations, both live and skeletal. Professionally investigating and restoring dinosaurs for three decades, Paul received an on-screen credit as a dinosaur specialist on *Jurassic Park* and Discovery Channel's *When Dinosaurs Roamed America* and *Dinosaur Planet*. He is the author and illustrator of *Predatory Dinosaurs of the World* (1988), *The Complete Illustrated Guide to Dinosaur Skeletons* (1996), *Dinosaurs of the Air* (2001), *The Princeton Field Guide To Dinosaurs* (2010), *Gregory S. Paul's Dinosaur Coffee Table Book* (2010), and editor of *The Scientific American Book of Dinosaurs* (2000). Paul has named over twelve prehistoric animal species and has had two dinosaur species named after him (*Cryptovolans pauli* and *Sellacoxa pauli*) based on his innovative theories.